Cover design: Foteini Belliou

First edition 2024

ISBN: 9781917613491

The images featured in the artistic synthesis of the book cover are sourced from Wikimedia Commons. They include: (a) Christ Pantocrator of Saint Catherine's Monastery (Sinai) and (b) The School of Athens by Raphael, located in Vatican City.

ANCIENT GREEK PHILOSOPHERS
The Christians before Christ

Vassileios Bellios

Translated By: Elena Kladi

To my wife, Anastasia and my children,

Spyros, Foteini and Nikos

TABLE OF CONTENTS

INTRODUCTION

«Ἐλήλυθεν ἡ ὥρα ἵνα δοξασθῇ ὁ υἱὸς τοῦ ἀνθρώπου»
(Ιω. ιβ΄23).

"The hour has come for the Son of Man to be glorified"
(John 12:23).

It is widely known that the heritage we have acquired from the Greek ancient ancestors is invaluable. Greece is popular worldwide due to its Ancient Greek Civilization. "The glorious city" («Τὸ κλεινὸν ἄστυ»), known as Athens, provided high-level education to the Greek youth especially from the early 4th century BCE, with the establishment of the *Platonic Academy* in 380 BCE, the *Lyceum* or *Peripatos* of Aristotle in 335 BCE, the *Garden of Epicurus* in 306 BCE, and the *Stoa Poikile of Zeno* in 300 BCE. All of these four philosophical schools were highly renowned, they were private and competed amongst themselves to attract the most students. They even sent criers to the ports of Pireaus and Sounion to attract newly arrived students who arrived by ships from other cities of the then-known world. The affluence and reputation of the city of Athens were also owed to the large number of prosperous students who came to Athens for their studies. According to Diogenes Laërtius their number was estimated to be around 2.000 (Diogenes Laërtius 5,37).

Christian theology was developed in this cultural climate, utilizing forms and concepts from ancient Greek philosophy. The degree of acceptance of the ancient heritage is reflected in the fact that ancient Greek philosophers are depicted alongside Orthodox Christian saints (such as Plato, Aristotle, Thucydides, Plutarch) in iconography. This is observed in monasteries like the Great Lavra (or Megisti Lavra), Iviron Monastery, Golas Monastery, and the Monastery of Saint Nicholas Philanthropinon.

The direct relationship between ancient Greek and Christian literature was studied by Saint Nektarios (Kefalas), Metropolitan of Pentapolis, in his work titled 'Treasury of Sacred and Philosophical Discourses', a text which has been consulted for the purposes of this book. He even writes that, while studying the ancient philosophers, he was convinced that: *"The Greek sages, in whole and in part, were teachers of truth, that they were lovers and seekers of truth, and that the love for the knowledge of truth led them towards true philosophy."*

This current endeavor is an amateur attempt to approach the vast treasure of Ancient Greek Literature, guided by the Christian tradition. It focuses on the converging points of the two traditions, juxtaposing the relevant excerpts to make them more readily accessible to the general audience. Representatives of Ancient Greek Literature are presented in alphabetical order, along with the relevance of their teachings to Christianity.

For those with a particular focus, there are relevant publications by specialists.

V.B.

1. Alcidamas (4th century BCE)

Alcidamas of Elaea (from Elaea in Aeolis, Asia Minor), a sophist and teacher of the art of rhetoric, lived in the 4th century BCE. He was the son of Diocles, a composer of musical works. Alcidamas studied under the rhetorician Gorgias of Leontini and he was the one who continued and expanded upon the theories on rhetoric that he acquired from his teacher. The primary goal of his teaching was to enable his students to speak impromptu and extemporaneously. Alcidamas surpassed his era, advocating for the Freedom and Equality of all people, including women, based on natural law. Unfortunately, his Messenian Speech has not been fully preserved.

Α «Ἐλευθέρους ἀφῆκε πάντας Θεός, οὐδένα δοῦλον ἡ φύσις πεποίηκεν» (Ancient Greek maxims, Μπαρακλῆς Χ., Γνωμικά καὶ Παροιμίες, σελ. 76).
"God let all people go free; nature has made no one a slave." (Baraklis Ch., Proverbs and Sayings, p.76).

† «Οὐκ ἔνι Ἰουδαῖος οὐδὲ Ἕλλην, οὐκ ἔνι δοῦλος οὐδὲ ἐλεύθερος, οὐκ ἔνι ἄρσεν καὶ θῆλυ. Πάντες γὰρ ὑμεῖς εἷς ἐστε ἐν Χριστῷ Ἰησοῦ» (Γαλ. Γ΄ 28).
"There is neither Jew nor Greek, there is neither slave nor free, there is no male and female, for you are all one in Christ Jesus" (Holy Scripture, Galatians 3:28).

2. Archilochus of Paros (680-630 BCE)

Ancient lyric poet who was born on Paros and reached the peak of his fame around 650 BCE. His father, Telesicles, came from an aristocratic family and served as the leader of the colonial expedition to Thasos, imparting to Archilochus his bold character. His mother was the slave Enipo. Archilochus led a turbulent life and was forced to become a mercenary, participating in wars in Ionia, Thrace, Macedonia, and Euboea. He met his end in battle against the Naxians. Archilochus composed elegies, hymns, and poems in iambic and trochaic meter.

A «Τοῖς θεοῖς τίθει τὰ πάντα» (Γνωμικά).

"Leave everything to the will of the gods." (Gnomic).

† «Πᾶσαν τὴν ζωὴν ἡμῶν Χριστῷ τῷ Θεῷ παραθώμεθα» (Λειτουργικόν).

"Let us commit our whole life to Christ our God" (Liturgy).

3. Aristotle (384-322 BCE)

Aristotle was an ancient Greek philosopher who was born in Stagira, Chalkidiki. He was a student of Plato and his teachings dominated Western philosophical and scientific thought until the Scientific Revolution of the 17th century. Widely regarded as one of the greatest philosophers of all time, he also excelled as a naturalist, creator of Logic and was the foremost among the dialecticians of Antiquity. Aristotle was summoned by King Philip of Macedonia to educate Alexander the Great. Despite his extensive work (400 books, mostly in the form of dialogues), only forty-seven survived along with some fragments. In 335 BCE, he founded his own philosophical school in Athens, known as the Peripatetic School, named after Aristotle's habit of teaching while walking in the garden.

Α «Ἡ φιλία καθ' αὑτὴν αἱρετὴ εἶναι. Δοκεῖ δὲ ἐν τῷ φιλεῖν μᾶλλον ἢ ἐν τῷ φιλεῖσθαι εἶναι. Σημεῖον δ' αἱ μητέρες τῷ φιλεῖν χαίρουσαι ἀντιφιλεῖσθαι δ' οὐ ζητοῦσιν» (Ἠθικὰ Νικομάχεια 1159α, 26-30, πηγή: Wikibooks).

"Friendship, considered in itself, is desirable. It appears, however, that there is more joy in loving than in being loved. A sign of this is that mothers delight in loving rather than being loved in return." (Nicomachean Ethics 1159a, 26-30, source: Wikibooks).

† «Ἡ ἀγάπη οὐ ζητεῖ τὰ ἑαυτῆς» (Α' Κορ. 13, 5).

"[Love] does not insist on its own way." (1st Corinthians 13:5)

4. Bias of Priene (625-540 BCE)

From Priene in Ionia, the son of Teutamus, Bias was a poet. He was one of the Seven Sages of Ancient Greece, known for his justice and rhetorical skill. He was a selfless, just, temperate, and frugal man. In the courts, he always advocated for free, defending the unjustly accused citizens. When forced to condemn someone to death, he wept. Satyrus the Peripatetic, who wrote the biographies of the Sages, called Bias the "preeminent among the Seven." According to Satyrus, when Athenian fishermen caught a bronze tripod with the inscription "to the wise," they handed it over to him, considering him the wisest man. It is said that he liberated some women who had become slaves by paying their ransom. He educated them, provided dowries, and sent them back to their families in Messenia. Today, his ethical sayings and excerpts from his lyrical poem are preserved. He wrote the poem "On the Ionia in which manner would one be most fortunate" with 2,000 verses and many aphorisms.[1]

Α «Ὅ,τι ἂν ἀγαθὸν πράσσῃς, θεούς, μὴ σεαυτὸν αἰτιῶ» (*Γνωμικά*).

"Whatever good fortune befalls you, attribute it to the gods". (Gnomic).

✝ « Ἴσθι πεποιθὼς ἐν ὅλῃ καρδίᾳ ἐπὶ Θεῷ, ἐπὶ δὲ σοφίᾳ μὴ ἐπαίρου» (*Παροιμ. 3, 5*).

"Trust in the Lord with all your heart, and do not lean on your own understanding" (Proverbs 3:5).

✝ «Πᾶν δώρημα τέλειον ἄνωθέν ἐστι καταβαῖνον ἐκ Σοῦ τοῦ Πατρὸς τῶν φώτων» (*Ἰακώβου 1, 17- βλ. και Ὀπισθάμβωνον Ευχήν κατά τη Θεία Λειτουργία*).

"Every good gift and every perfect gift is from above, coming down from the Father of the heavenly lights" (James 1:17 see also the *Receiving Wish* of the Divine Mass).

5. Chilon of Sparta (or Lacedaemon) (620-520 BCE)

He was a Spartan statesman, lawmaker, philosopher, and

---

[1] «Περὶ Ἰωνίας τίνα μάλιστ' ἂν τρόπον εὐδαιμονοίη»

elegiac poet, listed among the Seven Sages of Ancient Greece. Born around 600 BCE in Sparta, he was regarded with honor and respect from his fellow citizens. He was even elected Ephor in 556 BCE during the 56th Olympiad. His tenure is considered highly successful and significant in the historical development of the city-state, as he proposed and successfully implemented the reforms associated with Lycurgus in the Spartan Constitution. This included the elevation of the institution of the Ephors and a decisive limitation of royal power and authority in favor of popular sovereignty. Although he composed approximately two hundred elegies, none have survived. However, several of his maxims such as notably "μηδέν άγαν" (nothing in excess), "γνῶθι σεαυτόν" (know thyself), and "ἐγγύα πάρα δ'άτα" (Make a pledge, and evil is nigh at hand), were preserved. The most significant among them were inscribed on the wall or frontispiece of the Temple of Apollo in Delphi.

A «Τὰ μὲν ὑψηλὰ ταπεινῶν, τὰ δὲ ταπεινὰ ὑψῶν» (Διογένης Λαέρτιος, Βίοι Φιλοσόφων Α 69).

"To humble the lofty and to elevate the humble." (Diogenes Laërtius, Lives of the Eminent Philosophers, A69). This was the response of Chilon of Sparta when asked by Aesop what Zeus is doing. («Ζεὺς τί εἴη ποιῶν;»).

† «Ὁ ὑψῶν ἑαυτὸν ταπεινωθήσεται, ὁ δὲ ταπεινῶν ἑαυτὸν ὑψωθήσεται» (Λουκ. 18, 14).

"For everyone who exalts himself will be humbled, but the one who humbles himself will be exalted." (Luke 18:14).

Ａ «Μὴ κακολογεῖν τοὺς πλησίον» (Διογ. Λαέρτ. Βίοι Φιλοσ. Α69).

"Do not speak ill of your neighbor." (Diogenes Laërtius, Lives of the Eminent Philosophers, A69).

† «Μὴ καταλαλεῖτε ἀλλήλων ἀδελφοί» (Επιστ. Ιακώβου 4. 11).

"Do not speak evil against one another brothers." (James 4:11).

6. Cleobulus of Rhodes (died around the late 6th century BCE)

One of the Seven Sages of Ancient Greece, Cleobulus, was the tyrant of Lindos and a poet. His aphorisms "Everything in moderation,"[2] "Be superior to pleasure,"[3] etc. are amongst the most well-known in ancient Greek sayings. He stood out for his strength and beauty. He traveled to Egypt and engaged in philosophy. As a poet, he composed hymns and riddles, which, according to Diogenes Laërtius, totaled 3,000 verses. Although ancient sources describe him as a tyrant, it seems that his rule benefited his city.

Ａ «Τὸν δὲ ἐχθρὸν φίλον ποιεῖν καὶ εὐεργετεῖν» (Διογ. Λαέρτ. Βίοι Φιλοσ. Α 91).

"Make your enemy a friend and be benevolent to him" (Diogenes Laërtius, Lives of the Eminent Philosophers, A91, Gnomic).

---

[2] «Μέτρον ἄριστον»

[3] «ἡδονῆς κράτει»

† «Ἀγαπᾶτε τοὺς ἐχθροὺς ὑμῶν» (Ματθ. 5,44).

"Love your enemies" (Matthew 5:44).

Α «Ἔχθραν διαλύειν» (Διογ. Λαέρτ. Βίοι Φιλοσ. Α,91,92, Γνωμικά).

"Dissolve the enmity you have with someone" (Diogenes Laërtius, Lives of the Eminent Philosophers, A91,92, Gnomic).

Α «Ὃ σὺ μισεῖς, ἑτέρῳ μὴ ποιήσῃς» (Γνωμικά).

"What is hateful to you, do not do to your neighbor" (Gnomic).

† «Πάντα ὅσα ἂν θέλητε ἵνα ποιῶσιν ὑμῖν οἱ ἄνθρωποι, οὕτω καὶ ὑμεῖς ποιεῖτε αὐτοῖς» (Ματθ. 7, 12).

"So whatever you wish that others would do to you, do also to them, for this is the Law and the Prophets." (Matthew 7:12).

7. Delphic Maxims

The 147 Delphics, also known as the Pythia Oracles, were concise sayings of few words each, attributed to the Seven Sages of ancient Greece: Thales of Miletus, Pittacus of Mytilene, Bias of Priene, Solon of Athens, Cleobulus of Rhodes, Periander of Corinth, and Chilon of Sparta.

These were wise instructions left to the Greeks by the sages of ancient Greece, forming a valuable legacy of knowledge and wisdom for future generations. They were inscribed on the front wall of the pronaos of the Temple of Apollo, on the door jambs of the gate of the great temple, on the lintel, or on the many columns placed around the temple. Pausanias wrote: "In the pronaos at Delphi are written maxims useful for the life of men"[4] (Phocian).

Here are some excerpts that resonate with the spirit of the Holy Scripture:

«Θεοὺς σέβου» - "Respect the gods"

«Γονεῖς αἰδοῦ» - "Honor your parents"

«Φόνου ἀπέχου» - "Abstain from murder"

«Ἕπου Θεῷ» - "Follow God"

«Ἁμαρτάνων μετανόει» - "Repent when you sin"

«Φθόνει μηδενί» - "Envy no one"

«Ἔχθρας διάλυε» - "Resolve conflicts with your enemies"

«Πλούτει δικαίως» - "Gain your wealth justly"

«Γλῶτταν ἴσχε» - "Guard your tongue"

«Ὅρκῳ μὴ χρῶ» - "Do not swear falsely"

«Ψέγε μηδένα» - "Speak ill of no one"

«Πρᾶττε δίκαια» - "Act justly"

«Ὕβριν μίσει» - "Hate hubris"

«Εὐλόγει πάντας» - "Speak well of all"

«Γλώττης ἄρχε» - "Control your speech"

«Ὀφθαλμοῦ κράτει» - "Guard your eyes"

«Ἀτυχοῦντι συνάχθου» - "Sympathize with the unfortunate"

«Τύχῃ μὴ πίστευε» - "Do not trust in fortune"

«Εὐγνώμων γίνου» - "Be grateful"

«Ὁμόνοιαν δίωκε» - "Pursue unity"

---

[4] «Ἐν δὲ τῷ προνάῳ τὰ ἐν Δελφοῖς γεγραμμένα ἐστὶν ὠφελήματα ἀνθρώποις»

8. Democritus of Abdera, Thrace (470-370 BCE)

Democritus, a Pre-Socratic philosopher born in Abdera, Thrace, was a disciple of Leucippus. He believed that matter is composed of indivisible, invisible elements known as atoms. He was the first to recognize that the Milky Way is the light from distant stars, and among the first to suggest that the universe has other "worlds" inhabited by beings. Democritus delved into nearly all areas of human knowledge. Later scholars in antiquity divided his extensive works into thirteen tetralogies, categorized into five groups: ethical (two tetralogies), natural (four tetralogies), mathematical (three), musical (two), and technical (two). Democritus' style was highly praised in antiquity, placing him on par with Plato and Aristotle. Only a few fragments of his vast writings have survived. A significant element of his ethical philosophy is the concept of *contentment*: one should be happy with what they have, and life should be organized according to moderation.

A «Εὐτυχὴς ὁ ἐπὶ μετρίοισι χρήμασι εὐθυμεόμενος, δυστυχὴς δὲ ὁ ἐπὶ πολλοῖσι δυσθυμεόμενος» (Στοβαίου Ανθολόγιον Τ 8216, Γνωμικά).

"Happy is the one who rejoices in moderate possessions; unhappy is the one who is discontented with many." (Florilegium of Stobaeus T 8216, Gnomic).

† «Πτωχός εἶναι ὁ τῶν πολλῶν ἐνδεής. Πλούσιος ὁ ἐν ὀλίγῳ ἀναπαυόμενος» (Πατερικόν).

"Poor is the one who needs many, and rich is the one who is content with little." (Patristic).

Α «Ἡδοναὶ ἄκαιροι τίκτουσιν ἀηδίας» (Γνωμικά).
"Untimely pleasures give birth to disgust" (Gnomic).

† «Πᾶσαν ἡδονὴν ἀκολουθεῖ ἀηδία καὶ πικρότης» (αγίου Ισαάκ του Σύρου, Συμβουλευτικοί λόγοι).
"After every pleasure, there comes displeasure and bitterness." (Saint Isaac the Syrian, Wise Counsels).

Α «Μοῦνοι θεοφιλέες, ὅσοις ἐχθρὸν τὸ ἀδικέειν» (Γνωμικά).
"The gods love only those who hate injustice." (Gnomic).

† «Κύριος ἀγαπᾶ δικαίους» (Ψαλμός 145, 8).
"The Lord is gracious and compassionate" (Psalm 145:8).

Α «Ἀγαθὸν οὐ τὸ μὴ ἀδικεῖν, ἀλλά τὸ μηδὲ θέλειν» (Γνωμικά).
"Virtue lies not only in not committing injustice but in not even desiring it." (Gnomic).

Α «Μὴ διὰ φόβον ἀλλὰ διὰ τὸ δέον ἀπέχεσθαι ἁμαρτημάτων» (Γνωμικά).
"Avoid sins not out of fear but out of a sense of duty." (Gnomic).

† "The Fathers of the Church say that people fall into three categories: a) those who work as slaves because they fear punishment, b) hired workers who expect their wages, and c) those who, out of love, do good. They do not exclude the first and the second from the Kingdom of God, but they praise the third.
(See Abba Dorotheos, Patrologia Graeca 88: 'We do good because

we fear punishment and then we are in the state of a slave, or to receive wages and then we are in the state of a hired worker, or for the sake of the good itself, and then we are in the state of a son. For the son does not do the will of his father out of fear, nor because he wants to receive wages from him, but because he wants to serve him, honor him, and give him rest. And thus, we should practice charity for virtue's sake, participating in the difficulties of others, as if they were members of our own body.')"

Α «Ἢν μὴ πολλῶν ἐπιθυμέῃς, τὰ ὀλίγα τοι πολλὰ δόξει» (Γνωμικά).

"If you do not desire many things, the few will seem much to you." (Gnomic).

† «Ζωή αυτάρκους εργάτου γλυκανθήσεται» (Σοφ. Σειράχ 40, 18).

"Life will be sweet for the self-reliant and the hardworking" (Sirach 40:18).

9. Epictetus (50-120 CE)

Epictetus was an Ancient Stoic philosopher. Tradition has it that he was born to enslaved parents in Hierapolis of Phrygia. Upon reaching Rome, he was purchased by Epaphroditus, a freedman of Nero, who subjected Epictetus to physical torment. He put his foot in a vise and tightened it to make him lose his patience. When Epictetus warned him, but Epaphroditus continued the squeezing until the harm occurred, Epictetus simply said, "Didn't I tell you that you would break my leg?"

During that period, Epictetus became interested in Stoic philosophy and summarized its principles in the phrase "sustain and abstain". After gaining his freedom, he settled in Rome briefly. After the persecutions of the philosophers under the decree of Domitian in 93 CE, he moved to Nicopolis in Epirus. There, he lived a humble and ascetic life, founding a philosophical school. Epictetus developed a philosophical system rooted in the ethics of Seneca. This was primarily a form of religious teaching that closely resembled Christianity. The focus of Epictetus' philosophy lies on human beings and their educational guidance, emphasizing ethics. Although Epictetus himself did not write, one of his students, Flavius Arrian, compiled his teachings into two works titled "The Discourses of Epictetus" and "The Enchiridion" or "Handbook". Epictetus is considered one of the prominent figures of the Late Stoa, the third period of Stoic philosophy, alongside Seneca and Marcus Aurelius.

Α «Ἀνέχου καὶ ἀπέχου» (Γνωμικά)
"Have patience and self-restraint." (Gnomic)

† «Ἐπιχορηγήσατε ἐν τῇ πίστει ὑμῶν τὴν ἀρετήν, ἐν δὲ τῇ ἀρετῇ τὴν γνῶσιν, ἐν δὲ τῇ γνώσει τὴν ἐγκράτειαν, ἐν δὲ τῇ ἐγκρατείᾳ τὴν ὑπομονήν, ἐν δὲ τῇ ὑπομονῇ τὴν εὐσέβειαν» (Β' Πέτρου, 1, 5-7).
"Make every effort to supplement your faith with virtue, and virtue with knowledge, and knowledge with self-control, and self-control with steadfastness, and steadfastness with godliness." (2 Peter, 1:5-7).

Α «Οὐδεὶς ἐλεύθερος ἑαυτοῦ μὴ κρατῶν». (Γνωμικά).
"No man is free who is not master of himself." (Gnomic).

† "When we are slaves to passions, our soul is dead." (Saint Isaac the Syrian, 205).

𝐀 «Υπάρχει Θεός που προνοεί για όλα και δεν είναι δυνατόν να δια- φύγουν την προσοχή του ούτε οι πράξεις μας, αλλά ούτε και οι προθέσεις και οι σκέψεις μας» (Διατριβαί Β', ιδ. 11)
"There is a God who cares for everything, and it is impossible for His attention to escape neither our actions nor our intentions and thoughts." (source: Baraklis, Ch., Proverbs and Sayings, p.274).

† «Οὐκ ἔστι κτίσις ἀφανὴς ἐνώπιον αὐτοῦ, πάντα δὲ γυμνὰ καὶ τετραχηλισμένα τοῖς ὀφθαλμοῖς αὐτοῦ» (Εβρ. 4, 13).
"Nothing in all creation is hidden from God's sight. Everything is uncovered and laid bare before the eyes of him to whom we must give account." (Hebrews 4:13).

𝐀 «Η αγάπη προς τους ανθρώπους είναι καθήκον, αφού είμαστε όλοι παιδιά του ίδιου Θεού» (Γνωμικά).
"Love for humanity is a duty, as we are all children of the same God." (Gnomic)

† «Ἀγαπῶμεν τὰ τέκνα τοῦ Θεοῦ, ὅταν τὸν Θεὸν ἀγαπῶμεν καὶ τὰς ἐντολὰς αὐτοῦ τηρῶμεν» (Α' Ιωάννου, 5:2).
"We know we love God's children if we love God and obey his commandments." (1 John 5:2).

† «Ταῦτα ἐντέλλομαι ὑμῖν ἵνα ἀγαπᾶτε ἀλλήλους» (Ιω. ιε',17).
"These things I command you that you will love one another."

(John 15:17).

Α «Σὺ (ἄνθρωπε) ἀπόσπασμα εἶ θεοῦ. Ἔχεις τι ἐν σε αυτῷ μέρος Ἐκείνου. Τί οὖν ἀγνοεῖς σου τὴν συγγένειαν;» (Διατριβαί 2,9,12).
"You are a fragment of God; you have within you a part of Him. Why, then, are you ignorant of your own kinship?" (The Discourses of Epictetus 2,9,12).

† «Οὐκ οἴδατε ὅτι τὸ σῶμα ὑμῶν ναὸς τοῦ ἐν ὑμῖν Ἁγίου Πνεύματός ἐστιν, οὗ ἔχετε ἀπὸ Θεοῦ, καὶ οὐκ ἐστὲ ἑαυτῶν;» (Α', Κορ. στ' 19).
"Or do you not know that your body is a temple of the Holy Spirit within you, whom you have from God? You are not your own;" (1 Corinthians 6:19).

Α «Δυσχερὲς πλουτοῦντα σωφρονεῖν» (Στοβαίου, 3.1.134).
"It is hard for those who are rich to be prudent." (Florilegium of Stobaeus 3.1.134).

† «Ἀμὴν λέγω ὑμῖν ὅτι δυσκόλως πλούσιος εἰσελεύσεται εἰς τὴν βασιλείαν τῶν οὐρανῶν» (Ματθ. 19, 23-24).
"Truly I say to you, only with difficulty will a rich person enter the Kingdom of Heaven." (Matthew 19:23-24).

10. Euripides (480-406 BCE)

Euripides was an ancient Greek tragic poet, one of the three great masters of Attic drama in ancient Greek theater. He hailed from the Athenian deme of Phlya, in present-day Chalandri.

Tradition has it that he was born in Salamis on the day of the naval battle, with Aeschylus fighting in the front line, and Sophocles as an adolescent leading the victory dance. His work reflects the spirit of the time, with a strong influence of sophistry, questioning, and the exploration of divine and human matters. Nineteen out of the eighty-one known works have survived to this day. The most well-known include "Electra," "Iphigenia," "Troades" (The Trojan Women or The Women of Troy), "Phoinissai" ("The Phoenician Women"), and "The Bacchae" also known as "The Bacchantes".

Α «Τά τοι μέγιστα πολλάκις θεὸς ταπειν᾽ ἔθηκε καὶ συνέστειλεν πάλιν» (Στοβαίου ΚΒ 32).

"God often humbles the very great and makes them low." (Florilegium of Stobaeus, 32).

† «Ὁ ὑψῶν ἑαυτὸν ταπεινωθήσεται ὁ δὲ ταπεινῶν ἑαυτὸν ὑψωθήσεται» (Λουκ. 18, 14).

"For everyone who exalts himself will be humbled, but the one who humbles himself will be exalted" (Luke 18:14).

Α «Θνητῶν ὄλβιος εἰς τὸ τέλος οὐδείς» (Γνωμικά).

"No mortal can be fortunate until his end" (Gnomic).

† «Ἐν τῷ κόσμῳ θλίψιν ἕξετε» (Ιω. ιστ᾽33).

"In the world you will have tribulation" (John 16:33).

Α «Τὰ τῶν τεκόντων ὡς μετέρχεται θεὸς μιάσματα» (Στοβαίου Ανθολόγιον ΙΑ᾽,15).

"God harshly punishes those who dishonor their parents." (Florilegium of Stobaeus 11:15).

† «Ὡς βλάσφημος ὁ ἐγκαταλείπων πατέρα καὶ κεκατηραμένος ὑπὸ Κυρίου ὁ παροργίζων μητέρα αὐτοῦ» (Σοφία Σειράχ 3, 16). "Those who abandon their fathers are like blasphemers, and those who anger their mothers have been cursed by the Lord" (Sirach 3:16).

A «Ὅστις δὲ τοὺς τεκόντας ἐν βίῳ σέβει, ὅδ' ἐστὶ καὶ ζῶν καὶ θανὼν θεοῖς φίλος» (Στοβαίου Ανθολόγιον ΙΑ' 2). "Whoever respects their parents in life, this one is a friend to the gods both in life and in death." (Stobaeus Florilegium, 11:2).

† «Ὁ τιμῶν πατέρα ἐξιλάσεται ἁμαρτίας καὶ ὡς ὁ ἀποθησαυρίζων, ὁ δοξάζων μητέρα αὐτοῦ». (Σοφία Σειράχ 3, 3-4). "Whoever honors his father atones for sins, and whoever glorifies his mother is like one who lays up treasure." (Sirach 3:3-4).

A «Εἰ θεοὶ εἰσὶ κακοί, οὐκ εἰσὶ θεοί» (Γνωμικά). "If the gods are evil, they are not gods" (Gnomic).

† «Οὐκ ἐστὶν αἴτιος τῶν κακῶν ὁ Θεός» (Μέγας Βασίλειος, PG 31,329A-353A). "God is not the cause of evils" (St. Basil the Great, PG 31,329A-353A).

† «Εὐεργέτην τεκοῦσα τὸν τῶν καλῶν αἴτιον» (Από την

Παράκληση της Παναγίας).

"You gave birth to our Benefactor, the Cause of all good." (From The Paraklesis: Supplication Prayer to the Mother of God).

A «Δεῖ φέρειν τὰ τῶν θεῶν» (Φοίνισσαι, Γνωμικά).

"We must bear what the gods send" (Phoenissae, Gnomic).

† «Ὁ δὲ ὑπομείνας εἰς τέλος οὗτος καὶ σωθήσεται» (Ματθ. ι',22).

"But the one who endures to the end will be saved" (Matthew 10:22).

† «Ἐν τῷ κόσμῳ θλίψιν ἕξετε, ἀλλὰ θαρσεῖτε, ἐγὼ νενίκηκα τὸν κόσμον» (Ιω. ιστ'. 33).

"In the world you will have tribulation. But take heart; I have overcome the world" (John 16:33).

A «Δεῖται γὰρ οὐδενός ὁ θεός, εἴπερ ἔστ'ὀρθῶς θεός» (Ηρακλής μαινόμενος, 1345, πηγή: Αγ. Νεκταρίου, Ἅπαντα, Η', σελ. 125).

"God needs nothing, if indeed He is truly God." (The Madness of Heracles, 1345, source: St. Nektarios, Apanta/Complete Works, vol. H', p.125).

† «Ἔλεον θέλω καὶ οὐ θυσίαν» (Ματθ. Θ', 13).

"I desire mercy, not sacrifice" (Matthew, 9:13).

A «Μισεῖ γὰρ ὁ θεὸς τὴν βίαν, τὰ κτητὰ δὲ κτᾶσθαι κελεύει πάντας οὐκ ἐς ἁρπαγάς» (Ελένη, Γνωμικά).

"For the god hates violence, and commands everyone to have

their possessions without robbery" (Helen, Gnomic).

† «Ἐμίσησας πάντας τοὺς ἐργαζομένους τὴν ἀνομίαν. Ἀπολεῖς πάντας τοὺς λαλοῦντας τὸ ψεῦδος. Ἄνδρα αἱμάτων καὶ δόλιον βδελύσσεται Κύριος» (Ψαλμ. ε΄ 6-7).
"You destroy those who speak lies; the LORD abhors the bloodthirstry and deceitful man" (Psalm 5:6-7).

Α «Οὐδεὶς θεὸς δύσνους ἀνθρώποις» (πηγή: Βικιβιβλία).
"No god is hostile to men" (source: Wikibooks).

† «Ὁ Θεὸς ἀγάπη ἐστί» (Α΄Ιω. 4:8).
"(Anyone who does not love does not know God, because) God is love" (1 John 4:8).

Α «Ἔστ᾽ ἀνδρὶ καὶ γυναικὶ κείμενος νόμος, τῷ μὲν διὰ τέλους ἦν ἔχει στέργειν ἀεί, τῇ δὲ ὅσ᾽ ἂν ἀρέσῃ τῷ ἀνδρὶ ταῦτα αὐτὴν ποιεῖν» (Εὐριπ. Frg. Inc.966, πηγή: Ἄννα Τζιροπούλου-Εὐσταθίου, Ἀρχαιογνωσία, αρ.φύλ. 22/75).
"There is a law established for both man and woman: for the man to cherish endlessly his wife, and for the woman to do whatever pleases her husband." (Euripides, Fragment Inc. 966, source: Anna Tziropoulou-Eustathiou, Archaeognosia, issue 22/75).

† «Ἕκαστος ἀγαπάτω τὴν ἑαυτοῦ γυναῖκα ὡς ἑαυτόν, ἡ δὲ γυνὴ ἵνα φοβῆται τὸν ἄνδρα» (Εφ. ε΄ 33).
"However, let each one of you love his wife as himself, and let the wife see that she respects her husband" (Ephesians 5:33).

𝐀 «Ἁμαρτεῖν εἰκὸς ἀνθρώπους» (Ἱππόλυτος, 615– βλ. Ἁγίου Νεκταρίου, Ἅπαντα, τόμ. Η΄, σελ.426).

"To err is human" (Hippolytus, 615 – see St. Nektarios, Apanta/Complete Works, vol. H', p.426).

† «Ουδείς αναμάρτητος...» (Κοντάκιον κεκοιμημέκων).

"No one is without sin." (Kontakion for the Departed).

𝐀 «Θυμὸς [...] μεγίστων αἴτιος κακῶν βροτοῖς» (Μήδεια, 1080– βλ. Ἁγίου Νεκταρίου, Ἅπαντα, τόμ. Η΄, σελ.343).

"Anger is the chief source of human woes." (Medea, 1080 – see St. Nektarios, Apanta/Complete Works, Vol. H', p. 343).

† «Μακάριοι οἱ πραεῖς, ὅτι αὐτοὶ κληρονομήσουσι τὴν γῆν» (Ματθ. ε΄5).

"Blessed are the meek, for they shall inherit the earth" (Matthew 5:5).

† «Ὀργὴ γὰρ ἀνδρὸς δικαιοσύνην Θεοῦ οὐ κατεργάζεται» (Ἰακώβου α΄ 20).

"For the anger of man does not produce the righteousness of God" (James 1:20).

𝐀 «Πάντα δ᾽ εὐπετῆ θεοῖς» (Φοίνισσαι, 689– βλ. Ἁγίου Νεκταρίου, Ἅπαντα, τόμ. Η΄, σελ.29).

"All things are easy for the gods" (Phoinissai, 689 – see St. Nektarios, Apanta/Complete Works, Vol. H', p. 29).

Α «Ζεύς μοι σύμμαχος , οὐ φοβοῦμαι» (Ἡρακλειδ. 766, βλ. Ἁγίου Νεκταρίου, Ἅπαντα, Η', σελ.29).

"Zeus is my ally; I am not afraid." (Heracleidae, 766– see St. Nektarios, Apanta/Complete Works, Vol. H', page 29).

† «Ἐγώ εἰμὶ μεθ' ὑμῶν καὶ οὐδεὶς καθ' ὑμῶν» (Κοντάκιον Ἀναλήψεως).

"I am with you, and no one is against you." (Kontakion of the Ascension).

11. Heraclitus, Ionian Philosopher (544-484 BCE)

Being a Presocratic philosopher who lived in the 6th to 5th century BCE in Ephesus, the second-largest city in Ionia, he was a descendant of the city's founder Androclus, born into an aristocratic family, independent and powerful, with a philosophical spirit. Approximately 130 fragments from his work have been preserved, and it is uncertain whether they originate from a single work. They are all brief, aphoristic, and enigmatic, following the pattern of Delphic oracles. Diogenes Laërtius attributes to Heraclitus a work titled 'On Nature.' Heraclitus had no students, did not establish a school, and was not interested in promoting his ideas. Nevertheless, his influence was significant for the development of ancient Greek and Western philosophical thought. Since antiquity, he has been called the 'dark philosopher' due to the interpretive difficulty of his works.

Α «Ἡδονή, μέγιστον κακοῦ δέλεαρ» (Γνωμικά).
"Pleasure, the greatest lure of evil" (Gnomic)

† "Pleasure is the greatest lure of evil, because of which people easily fall into sin." (St. Basil the Great, Moralia).

12. Hippocrates of Kos (460-370 BCE)

Hippocrates, an ancient Greek physician, is considered one of the most prominent figures in the history of medicine. He is referred to as 'the father of modern medicine'. Hippocrates laid the foundation for rational medicine, managing to free it from metaphysical elements, prejudices, preconceptions, demonologies, and superstitions of the time. He achieved a harmonious combination of human-centered science with medical art and philosophical contemplation, aligning professional practice with ethical-deontological principles and humanistic values. Dorian by origin, he was born around 460 BCE on the island of Kos and belonged to the illustrious Asclepiad family. According to tradition, Hippocrates was believed to trace his ancestry to the god of medicine, Asclepius, through his father Heraclides, who was also a physician. On his mother's side, he was said to have connections to the Greek mythological hero Heracles through his mother Phaenarete. Gifted with great diligence and a penchant for learning, he studied medicine at the renowned Asclepieion of Kos. Hippocrates traveled extensively to enhance his education and spread his belief in the healing power of pure air, water, and sunlight. His reputation spread rapidly throughout Greece and beyond its borders. Hippocrates passed away in Larissa around 377 BCE at the age of 83. He left behind 59 works, collectively known as the Hippocratic Corpus, written in Attic Greek (the Greek dialect of the ancient region of Attica). The Hippocratic Oath, believed to have been authored by Hippocrates and one of his students in the 4th century BCE, is taken by physicians and addresses the ethical principles of medical practice. It is also included in the Hippocratic Corpus.

Α «Πᾶν τὸ πολὺ τῇ φύσει πολέμιον» *(Γνωμικά)*.

"Everything in excess is opposed to nature." (Gnomic).

† «Βάρος ὑπὲρ σὲ μὴ ἄρῃς» *(Σοφία Σειράχ 13, 2)*.

"Do not lift a weight too heavy for you" (Sirach 13:2).

Α «Σιτία, ποτά, ὕπνος, αφροδίσια, πάντα μέτρια». (Στοβαίου Ανθολόγιο).

"Food, drinks, sleep, and sexual pleasures, all in moderation." (Stoveou Anthology).

† «Ἔλαμψε τῆς ἐγκρατείας ἡ εὐπρέπεια, τῶν δαιμόνων τὴν ἀχλὺν φυγαδεύουσα, ἐπεδήμησε τῆς νηστείας ἡ σεμνότης, τῶν ψυχικῶν παθῶν τὴν ἰατρείαν φέρουσα». *(Από την υμνολογία του Τριωδίου, της εβδομάδος της Τυρινής)*.

"The beauty of self-control has shone forth, dispelling the darkness of demons; the sobriety of fasting has revealed itself, bringing healing to the passions of the soul." (From the hymnography of the Triodion, of the week of Tyrophagus).

13. Homer, poet (est. 800-750 BCE)

Homer has been characterized as the greatest of all poets, marking the beginning of Greek and European literature. He is credited with creating the poetic texts of the Iliad and the Odyssey, known as the "Homeric Epics", among the earliest works of the historical period of ancient Greece. The Iliad consists of 15,693 verses and recounts the decisive events of the last fifty-one days of the Trojan War, a mythical conflict said to have lasted ten years. The Odyssey, with approximately 12,110 verses, narrates the ten-year struggle of Odysseus for his *nostos* (the return home to his homeland, Ithaca, after the capture of Troy). According to some commentators, the Iliad is considered the work of the poet's youth, contrasting with the Odyssey, which is viewed as a creation of his maturity. Homer's origin appears to be from Ionia—seven cities dispute his birthplace, with Smyrna and Chios being the prevailing contenders. It is said that his real name was Melisigenes[5], as he was born near the River Meles in Smyrna, and later took the name "Homer,"[6] either because he was blind[7] or because he was a hostage[8] of the Colophonians in the war against Smyrna. According to tradition, he traveled, reciting his works in Greek cities, and gained great fame.

A «Θεοί τε τὰ πάντα ἴσασιν» (Ὀδύσσεια, δ', στ. 379-381).
"For the gods know all things" (Odyssey, Book 4, line 380).

† «Μείζων ἐστὶν ὁ Θεὸς τῆς καρδίας ἡμῶν καὶ γινώσκει πάντα» (Ἐπιστολή Ἰω. γ'. 20).

---

[5] genes from the Greek verb "γεννῶ"- gennó

[6] Ὅμηρος – Homēros (in Greek phonology)

[7] «ὡς μὴ ὁρῶν» - "hōs mē horōn", which means the one who does not see in Greek

[8] another meaning of the word Homēros in Greek

"For whenever our heart condemns us, God is greater than our heart, and he knows everything. (Letter John 3:20).

A «Θεός δε τε πάντα δύναται» (Οδύσσεια, κ', στ. 306– βλ. Αγίου Νεκταρίου, Άπαντα, Η', σελ.29).

"But with the gods all things are possible" (Odyssey, Book 10, Line 306 – see St. Nektarios, Apanta/Complete Works, vol. H', p.29).

A «Πάντες δὲ θεῶν χατέουσ' ἄνθρωποι» (Οδύσσεια, γ', στ. 45-48).

"For all men have need of the gods" (Odyssey, Book 3, lines 45-48).

† «Ὃς πάντας ἀνθρώπους θέλει σωθῆναι καὶ εἰς ἐπίγνωσιν ἀληθείας ἐλθεῖν» (Τιμ. Α',2,4).

"(He) who desires all people to be saved and to come to the knowledge of the truth" (1 Timothy 2:4).

A «Θεῶν ἐν γούνασι κεῖται» (Ἰλιάδα, Ρ, στ. 514).

"The outcome of an effort lies on the knees of the gods." (Iliad, Book 17, line 514).

† «Ἐὰν μὴ Κύριος οἰκοδομήσῃ οἶκον, εἰς μάτην ἐκοπίασαν οἱ οἰκοδομοῦντες, ἐὰν μὴ Κύριος φυλάξῃ πόλιν, εἰς μάτην ἠγρύπνησεν ὁ φυλάσσων» (Ψαλμ. 126,1).

"Unless the LORD builds the house, those who build it labor in vain. Unless the LORD watches over the city, the watchman stays awake in vain." (Psalm 127:1).

Α «Φιλοφροσύνη γὰρ ἀμείνων. Ληγέμεναι δ' ἔριδος κακομηχάνου...» (Ιλιάδα, Ι, στ. 257-258).

"Gentle-mindedness is the better part, and withdraw yourself from strife, contriver of mischief." (Iliad, Book 9, lines 257-258).

✝ «Η αγάπη μακροθυμεί, χρηστεύεται, ου ζηλοί, η αγάπη ου περπερεύεται, ου φυσιούται, ουκ ασχημονεί, ου ζητεί τα εαυτής, ου παροξύνεται, ου λογίζεται το κακόν, ου χαίρει επί τη αδικία, συγχαίρει δε τη αληθεία. Πάντα στέγει, πάντα πιστεύει, πάντα ελπίζει, πάντα υπομένει. Η αγάπη ουδέποτε εκπίπτει» («Ύμνος της Αγάπης», Παύλου, Α' Κορ., ΙΓ', 4-8).

"Love is patient and kind; love does not envy or boast; it is not arrogant or rude. It does not insist on its own way; it is not irritable or resentful; it does not rejoice at wrongdoing, but rejoices with the truth. Love bears all things, believes all things, hopes all things, endures all things. Love never ends." (1 Corinthians 13:4-8).

14. Isocrates (436-338 BCE)

Isocrates was an ancient Greek rhetorician, one of the ten Attic orators. Born into a wealthy family, he received the best possible education and studied under several sophists, as well as Socrates. He was one of the most significant rhetoric instructors of classical antiquity and is considered a figure who influenced the political situation of his time. His involvement in public affairs was indirect, using his speeches to intervene in the politics of Athens by expressing panhellenic ideas. While advocating for the conquest of barbarian nations in foreign policy, he preferred democracy over oligarchy in domestic matters, he praised Pericles, but admired Solon. Twenty-one of his speeches, five letters, and some other fragments are preserved.

Α «Ζεὺς ὁ κρατῶν πάντων» (Ελένης Εγκώμιον).
"Zeus, the ruler of all" (Encomium of Helen).

† «Πιστεύω εἰς ἕνα Θεόν, Πατέρα παντοκράτορα» (Σύμβολο της Πίστεως).
"I believe in one God, the Father Almighty" (The Nicene Creed).

† «Σήμερον γεννᾶται ἐκ παρθένου ὁ δρακὶ τὴν πᾶσαν ἔχων κτίσιν» (από την Ακολουθίαν των Ωρών των Χριστουγέννων).

"Today, He who holds the whole creation in His hand is born of a Virgin." (From The Byzantine Hymn of the Nativity).

† «Καὶ γὰρ ὄντως ἐξανέτειλεν ἐκ Σοῦ ὁ Κύριος ὁ δρακὶ συνέχων τὰ πέρατα» (από την υμνολογία του Πεντηκοσταρίου, Αγίων Πατέρων).
"For indeed, the Lord, who holds the ends of the earth in His grasp, has truly risen from You" (from the hymnography of Pentecost, Holy Fathers).

15. Menander of Athens (342-291 BCE)

Menander was an Athenian comic playwright, a master and the best-known representative of the genre called Athenian New Comedy. This genre depicted everyday people in ordinary situations, in contrast to Old Comedy, which had political or fantastical content. As a teenager, Menander studied at Aristotle's

Peripatetic School. He wrote around 100 comedies, and his work influenced later Roman writers like Plautus and Terence, as well as comedy in the West after the Renaissance. Menander's reputation has grown with new discoveries of fragments from his works on Oxyrhynchus Papyri. He is also credited with the anthology of maxims known as *"Gnomai monostichoi* or *Sententiae,"* which was considered an instructional book for many centuries. Only one complete play, "Dyscolus" ("The Grouch"), has survived, but substantial portions of "Epitrepontes" ("The Arbitration"), "Samia" ("The Girl from Samos") and *"Perikeiromenē"* ("The Shorn Girl") are also extant.

Α «Φόβος τὰ θεῖα τοῖσι σώφροσι βροτῶν» (Στοβαίου Ανθολόγιον).

"Wise people respect the gods." (Florilegium of Stobaeus).

✝ «Μετὰ φόβου Θεοῦ πίστεως καὶ ἀγάπης προσέλθετε» (Λειτουργικόν).

"In the fear of God, with faith and love draw near." (Liturgy).

✝ «...καὶ τῶν μετά πίστεως εὐλαβείας καὶ φόβου Θεοῦ εἰσιόντων ἐν αὐτῷ τοῦ Κυρίου δεηθῶμεν» (Λειτουργικόν).

"...and for those who enter this holy house with faith, reverence, and the fear of God, let us pray to the Lord" (Liturgy).

Α «Ἔστι δίκης ὀφθαλμός, ὃς τὰ πάνθ' ὁρᾷ» (Γνωμικά).

"The eye of Justice sees all things." (Gnomic).

† «Ὀφθαλμοὶ Κυρίου ἐπὶ δικαίους καὶ ὦτα αὐτοῦ εἰς δέησιν αὐτῶν» (Ψαλμ. λγ΄16).

"The eyes of the Lord are on the righteous, and His ears are attentive to their cry." (Psalm 34:16).

Α «Ἀγάπης οὐδὲν μεῖζον οὔτε ἴσον ἐστί» (Γνωμικά).

"There is nothing greater or equal to love." (Gnomic).

† «Ἡ ἀγάπη μακροθυμεῖ, χρηστεύεται, οὐ ζηλοῖ, οὐ περπερεύεται, οὐ φυσιοῦται, οὐκ ἀσχημονεῖ, οὐ ζητεῖ τὰ ἑαυτῆς, οὐ παροξύνεται, οὐ λογίζεται τὸ κακόν, οὐ χαίρει ἐπὶ τῇ ἀδικίᾳ, συγχαίρει δὲ τῇ ἀληθείᾳ. Πάντα στέγει, πάντα πιστεύει, πάντα ἐλπίζει, πάντα ὑπομένει. Ἡ ἀγάπη οὐδέποτε ἐκπίπτει»). («Ὕμνος της Αγάπης», Παύλου, Α΄ Κορ. ΙΓ΄, 4-8).

"Love is patient and kind; love does not envy or boast; it is not arrogant or rude. It does not insist on its own way; it is not irritable or resentful; it does not rejoice at wrongdoing, but rejoices with the truth. Love bears all things, believes all things, hopes all things, endures all things. Love never ends." (1 Corinthians 13:4-8).

Α «Ὀξὺς θεῶν ὀφθαλμὸς ἐς τὸ πάνθ᾽ ὁρᾶν» (Γνωμικά).
"The sharp eye of the gods sees everything." (Gnomic).

Α «Θεοὺς σέβου καὶ πάντα πράξεις ἐνθέως» (Γνωμικά).
"Worship the gods, and you will live a godly life in all your actions." (Gnomic).

† «Τοῖς ἀγαπῶσι τὸν Θεὸν πάντα συνεργεῖ εἰς ἀγαθὸν» (Ρωμ. 8,

28).

"All things work together for good to them that love God" (Romans 8:28).

Α «Δίκαια δράσας, συμμάχους ἕξεις θεούς» (Γνωμικά).

"Act justly, and you will have the gods as allies." (Gnomic).

† «Ὁ πορευόμενος δικαίως βεβοήθηται» (Παροιμ. 28.18).

"Whoever walks in integrity will be delivered" (Proverbs 28:18)

Α «Θεὸς συνεργός, πάντα ποιεῖ ῥαδίως» (Γνωμικά).

"God, as a collaborator, effortlessly accomplishes everything." (Gnomic).

† «Κύριος στερέωμά μου καὶ καταφυγή μου καὶ ῥύστης μου» (Ψαλμ. ιζ' 3).

"The Lord is my rock, my fortress and my deliverer;" (Psalm 18:2).

† «Ἐγώ εἰμὶ μεθ' ὑμῶν καὶ οὐδεὶς καθ' ὑμῶν» (Κοντάκιον Ἀναλήψεως).

"I am with you, and no one is against you." (Kontakion of the Ascension).

† «Μετά φόβου Θεοῦ πίστεως καὶ ἀγάπης προσέλθετε» (Λειτουργικόν).

"In the fear of God, with faith and love draw near." (Liturgy).

16. Phocylides of Miletus (late 6th-early 5th century BCE)

A gnomic poet from Miletus, who flourished around 537 BCE. He composed ethical precepts (gnomic verses) in hexameters and distichs, beginning them consistently with the following three words: "And this from Phocylides." This is why he was also called a gnomic poet. While the gnomic verses he wrote have not been preserved as a complete work, they are scattered in references by other authors. Following the example of Hesiod, he praised agriculture as the most commendable profession (Fragment 7D), advised one to be prudent and just, recommended avoiding recklessness, and, in another fragment, spoke about the wickedness of women. His collection of maxims served as a guide for everyday life, written in simple language. He engaged in poetic exchanges with his contemporary Demodocus from Leros who was also a poet.

Α « Ὅλους ἀγάπα» (Γνωμικά).
"Love everyone." (Gnomic).

† «Ἀγαπᾶτε ἀλλήλους» (Ἰω. ιε′17).
"Love one another." (John 13:34).

Α «Μήτε γαμοκλοπέειν, μήτ᾽ ἄρσενα Κύπριν ὀρίνειν» (Γνωμικά).
"Neither commit adultery, nor turn to a male (homosexual) love." (Gnomic).

† «Οὐ μοιχεύσεις» (6η Εντολή).

"You shall not commit adultery" (6th Commandment).

A «Παιδὸς δ' εὐμόρφου φρουρεῖν νεοτήσιον ὥρην, πολλοὶ γὰρ λυσσῶσι πρὸς ἄρσενα μεῖξιν ἔρωτος» (Γνωμικά).
"Be cautious, protecting the adolescent age of a beautiful child, for many are frenzied for a carnal union with a male." (Gnomic).

† «Μὴ πλανᾶσθε, οὔτε πόρνοι, οὔτε εἰδωλολάτραι, οὔτε μοιχοί, οὔτε μαλακοί, οὔτε ἀρσενοκοῖται, οὔτε πλεονέκται, οὔτε κλέπται, οὔτε μέθυσοι, οὐ λοίδοροι, οὐχ ἄρπαγες βασιλείαν Θεοῦ οὐ κληρονομήσουσι» (Α' Κορινθ., στ'. 9-10).
"Do not be deceived: neither the sexually immoral, nor idolaters, nor adulterers, nor men who practice homosexuality, nor thieves, nor the greedy, nor drunkards, nor revilers, nor swindlers will inherit the kingdom of God." (1 Corinthians 6:9-10).

17.Pittacus of Mytilene (650-570 BCE)

Pittacus was a political and military leader of Mytilene and one of the Seven Sages of Ancient Greece. Mytilene is referred to as his place of origin. He was renowned for his political and social wisdom, his clear and just legislation, his prudence, kindness, and military courage. He entered the political arena of his homeland in 612 BCE and led his fellow citizens in a war against the Athenians, aiming to occupy the Sigeion in the Troad, an ancient colony of Mytilene at the mouth of the Hellespont. Pittacus distinguished himself in battle and even killed Phrynon, an Athenian general and Olympic victor famous for his courage and bravery, in single combat. The people of Mytilene honored him for his achievements, but he accepted only the land marked by the throw of his spear. He dedicated the land to sacred use, known as the Land of Pittacus. Internal disturbances arose in Mytilene, instigated by aristocrats led by Alcaeus and his brother Antimenides. When they were exiled, Mytilene experienced a period of relative calm until the exiles attempted to return by force of arms. To counter the threat, the people chose Pittacus as the "aisymnētēs" (chosen tyrant) and granted him absolute power. He remained in power for a decade (589-579), and after its expiration, he voluntarily resigned from the position of authority. Pittacus is credited with many elegiac poems, which are not preserved, and numerous maxims. His most famous maxim is "Know thine opportunity" («καιρόν γνῶθι»).

𝐀 «Καλλιέργησε την αγάπη και τη φιλία με έναν εχθρό» (Γνωμικά).
"Cultivate love and friendship with an enemy." (Gnomic).

† «Ἀγαπᾶτε τοὺς ἐχθροὺς ὑμῶν» (Λουκά 6:27)
"Love your enemies" (Loukas 6:27).

𝐀 «Συγγνώμη τιμωρίας κρείσσων» (Διογ. Λαέρτιος, Βίοι Φιλοσόφων, Α,76, Γνωμικά)
"Forgiveness is better than revenge." (Diogenes Laërtius, Lives of the Eminent Philosophers, A76, Gnomic).
"He forgave the murderer of his son! The Greek tradition has preserved a story that, for some, illustrates the magnanimity and kindness of Pittacus, while for others, it suggests that he did not seek revenge and did not uphold the laws he proclaimed, arguing that he should have punished the ironworker with death. Once,

Pittacus's son Tyrrhaeus, while sitting in a barber shop in Cumae, was killed by an ironworker with an axe. The residents of Cumae captured the murderer and brought him to Pittacus. After hearing the account of the incident, Pittacus released him, saying: 'Forgiveness is better than revenge'.

† «...ὡς καὶ ἡμεῖς ἀφίεμεν τοῖς ὀφειλέταις ἡμῶν...» (Κυριακή Προσευχή).

"...as we also forgive our debtors..." (The Lord's Prayer).

Α «Ἀγάπα τὸν πλησίον σου, μικρὰ ἐλαττούμενος» (Στοβαίου Ἀνθολόγιον, Γνωμικά).

"Love your neighbor, even if it means diminishing or harming yourself a little." (Florilegium of Stobaeus, Gnomic).

† Saint Dionysius of Zakynthos (1547-1622) forgave his brother's murderer, Constantine. Despite his grief, he not only concealed the killer but also helped him escape. In this way, he managed to offer the murderer the opportunity to repent, setting an example of forgiveness and the profound practice of Christian love (Nicodemus the Hagiorite: Synaxarist of the twelve months of the year, Volume A).

18. Plato, the Athenian (427-347 BCE)

Plato was an ancient Athenian philosopher, renowned as the most famous disciple of Socrates and the teacher of Aristotle. His dedication to Socrates is unparalleled in the history of student-teacher relationships. He earned the name Plato, meaning 'broad' or 'wide,' likely in reference to the breadth of his chest and forehead. His work, presented in the form of philosophical dialogues, has been preserved in its entirety and significantly influenced ancient Greek philosophy and, more broadly, the Western philosophical tradition up to the present day. Amongst his notable works are the 'Apology of Socrates,' 'Symposium' discussing the nature of love, and two extensive dialogues, 'The Republic' and 'The Laws,' describing the ideal state. Plato authored a total of 36 works, all in dialogue format. In addition to his philosophical contributions, he founded the famous Academy, named after the location dedicated to the hero Academus (or Hecademus), where Plato taught for 42 years.

A «Ὁ Θεὸς οὐδαμῇ, οὐδαμῶς ἄδικος» (Θεαίτητος 176c, Γνωμικά). "God is in no wise and in no manner unrighteous" (Theaetetus 176c, Gnomic).

† «Ἡ κρίσις ἡ ἐμὴ δικαία ἐστί» (Ἰωάν. ε′ 30).
"And my judgement is just" (John, 5:30).

† «Ὁ Θεὸς Κριτὴς δίκαιος καὶ ἰσχυρὸς καὶ μακρόθυμος καὶ μὴ ὀργὴν ἐπάγων καθ' ἑκάστην ἡμέραν» (Ψαλμ. ζ′,12).
"God is a righteous judge and a God who feels indignation every day" (Psalm 7:11).

A «Τέλος μὲν εἶναι τὴν ἐξομοίωσιν τῷ Θεῷ» (Διογ. Λαέρτιος, Βίοι Φιλοσόφων Γ 78).
"To resemble God is the ultimate end." (Diogenes Laertius, Lives of the Eminent Philosophers, 3, 78).

† "Theosis is the purpose of human life. According to the Holy Fathers, the prerequisites are humility, asceticism, the Mysteries of the Church, and prayer." (Abbot George Kapsanis of the Holy Monastery of St. Gregorios, Mount Athos, 2007).

Α «τί τὸ ὂν ἀεί, γένεσιν δὲ οὐκ ἔχον» (Τίμαιος 5, 27d).
"That which is eternal has no genesis." (Timaeus 5, 27d).

Α «Ψυχὴ πᾶσα ἀθάνατος» (Φαίδρος, Γνωμικά, πηγή: Μπαρακλῆς Χ. σελ.192).
"Every soul is immortal." (Phaedrus, Gnomic, source: Baraklis Ch., p.192).

† «Οὐχ ἡ ψυχὴ ἐστὶν ἡ ἀποθνήσκουσα ἀλλὰ διὰ τὴν ταύτης ἀναχώρησιν ἀποθνήσκει τὸ σῶμα» (Μ. Ἀθανάσιος).
"It is not the soul that dies. Instead, because the soul departs from the body, that is why a person dies." (St. Athanasius).

Α «Ὁ μὲν δὴ Θεός, ὥσπερ καὶ ὁ παλαιὸς λόγος, ἀρχήν τε καὶ τελευτὴν καὶ μέσα τῶν ὄντων ἁπάντων ἔχει» (Νόμοι Δ 7,15 Ε).
"Indeed, God, as the ancient saying goes, holds the beginning, end, and middle of all things." (Laws, D 7:15).

† "We believe in one God, an unoriginate, beginningless, and ineffable Principle, unborn, unalterable, and immutable, infinite Source of all that exists." - St. John of Damascus.

Α «Πᾶς ὅ τ᾽ ἐπὶ γῆς καὶ ὑπὸ γῆς χρυσὸς ἀρετῆς οὐκ ἀντάξιος»

(Νόμοι, Ε 728 α).

"All the gold on earth and under the earth is not worth as much as virtue." (Laws, E 728a).

† «Ὅσον οὖν πλεονάζεις τῷ πλούτῳ, τοσοῦτον ἐλλείπεις τῇ ἀγάπῃ» (Μ. Βασίλειος, «Πρὸς τοῦ Πλουτοῦντας», 52c).

"For the more you abound in wealth, the more you lack in love" (St. Basil the Great, "Sermon to the Rich", 52c).

Α «Αἰτία ἑλομένου, Θεὸς ἀναίτιος» (Γνωμικά).

"The blame is his who chooses: God is blameless" (Gnomic).

† «Μηδεὶς πειραζόμενος λεγέτω ὅτι ἀπὸ τοῦ Θεοῦ πειράζομαι. Ὁ γὰρ Θεὸς ἀπείραστός ἐστιν κακῶν, πειράζει γὰρ αὐτὸς οὐδένα» (Ἐπιστολή Ἰακώβου 1, 13-15).

"Let no one say when he is tempted, "I am being tempted by God", for God cannot be tempted with evil, and he himself tempts no one." (James 1:13-15).

Α «Μᾶλλον ἀδικεῖσθαι ἢ ἀδικεῖν» (Γνωμικά).

"Better to be wronged than to wrong." (Gnomic).

† «... διατί οὐχὶ μᾶλλον ἀδικεῖσθε; διατί οὐχὶ μᾶλλον ἀποστερεῖσθε; (Α′ Κορ. στ′ 7).

"Why not rather suffer wrong? Why not rather be defrauded?" (1 Corinthians 6:7).

Α «Ὁ θάνατος τυγχάνει ὢν, ὡς ἐμοὶ δοκεῖ, οὐδὲν ἄλλο ἢ δυοῖν

πραγμάτοιν διάλυσις, τῆς ψυχῆς καὶ τοῦ σώματος ἀπ' ἀλλήλου» (Γνωμικά).

"Death, as it seems to me, is actually nothing but the disconnection of two things, the soul and the body, from each other." (Gnomic).

† «Ὄντως φοβερώτατον τὸ τοῦ θανάτου μυστήριον, πῶς ψυχὴ ἐκ τοῦ σώματος βιαίως χωρίζεται ἐκ τῆς ἁρμονίας, καὶ τῆς συμφυΐας ὁ φυσικώτατος δεσμὸς θείῳ βουλήματι ἀποτέμνεται» (Νεκρώσιμον).

"Truly, the mystery of death is most awe-inspiring, how the soul is forcibly separated from the body, breaking the natural bond of harmony and unity by divine will." (Funeral service).

Α «Εἰσὶ γὰρ δὴ οἱ περί τὰς τελετὰς ναρθηκοφόροι μὲν πολλοί, βάκχοι δέ τε παῦροι» (Φαίδων, 69 C).

"For as they say in the [Eleusinian] mysteries, 'the thyrsus-bearers are many, but the mystics few'". (Phaedo, 69c).

† «Πολλοὶ οἱ κλητοὶ ὀλίγοι οἱ ἐκλεκτοί» (Ματθ. κβ',14).

"For many are called, but few are chosen" (Matthew 22:14).

Α «Οὔκ εἰσιν οἱ παμπλούσιοι ἀγαθοί» (Νόμοι 743c, πηγή: Αγ. Νεκτάριου, Ἅπαντα, Η', σ. 222).

"Those who are excessively rich are not necessarily virtuous" (Laws 743c, source: St. Nektarios, Apanta/Complete Works, vol. H', p.222).

† «Εὐκοπώτερόν ἐστι κάμηλον διὰ τρυπήματος ῥαφίδος διελθεῖν, ἢ πλούσιον εἰς τὴν βασιλείαν τοῦ Θεοῦ εἰσελθεῖν» (Ματθ. 19. 19-24.)

"It is easier for a camel to go through the eye of a needle than for a rich person to enter the kingdom of God" (Matthew 19:19-24).

19.Plutarch (47-120 CE)

A great historian, philosopher, biographer, and essayist, but above all, he was the chief priest and supervisor of Delphi. He lived the majority of his life in Chaeronea, where he founded a philosophical school emphasizing the teaching of ethics as a way of life. He was also responsible for interpreting the Pythian Oracles, a position he held for 29 years until his death. For Plutarch, knowledge of history was a primary and essential asset for those aspiring to engage in politics. He led a particularly active social and political life, during which he produced a large number of texts that have survived to the present day. His most significant works include the classical 'Parallel Lives' (biographies with an educational purpose) and the 'Moralia' (a collection of essays and treatises covering a wide range of topics, such as religion, metaphysics, history, politics, music, and philology).

Α «Θηρίον ἐστὶ δουλαγωγὸν ἡ ἡδονή» (Στοβαίου Ανθολόγιον).
"Pleasure is a beast that enslaves" (Florilegium of Stobaeus).

† «Πᾶν τὸ ἐν τῷ κόσμω, ἡ ἐπιθυμία τῆς σαρκὸς καὶ ἡ ἐπιθυμία τῶν ὀφθαλμῶν καὶ ἡ ἀλαζονεία τοῦ βίου, οὐκ ἐκ τοῦ πατρός, ἀλλ' ἐκ τοῦ κόσμου ἐστί» (Α' Ιω. 2, 6).
"For all that is in the world- the desires of the flesh, and the desires

of the eyes and pride of life- is not from the Father but is from the world" (1 John 2:16).

Α «Ὁ μὴ νομίζων Θεὸν ἀνόσιός ἐστι» (Ηθικά, 169 F).

"He who does not believe in God is impious." (Ethics, 169F).

† «Εἶπεν ἄφρων ἐν τῇ καρδίᾳ αὐτοῦ, Οὐκ ἔστι Θεός» (Ψαλμ, νβ΄,2).

"The fool says in his heart, there is no God" (Psalm 53:1).

Α «Εὕροις δ' ἂν ἐπιὼν πόλεις ἀτειχίστους, ἀγραμμάτους, ἀβασιλεύτους, ἀοίκους, ἀχρημάτους, νομίσματος μὴ δεομένας, ἀπείρους θεάτρων καὶ γυμναστηρίων. Ἀνιέρου δὲ πόλεως καὶ ἀθέου, μὴ χρωμένης εὐχαῖς, μηδ' ὅρκοις, μηδὲ μαντείαις, μηδὲ θυσίαις ἐπ' ἀγαθοῖς, μηδ' ἀποτροπαῖς κακῶν οὐδείς ἐστι, οὐδ' ἔσται γεγονὼς θεατής» (Γνωμικολογικόν- Βιβλιοθήκη των Ελλήνων, τόμος 2ος, εκδ. Ελληνικός Εκδοτικός Οργανισμός, Αθήναι 1972, σελ.31).

"In your wanderings, you may encounter cities without walls, without a writing system, without kings, without houses, without possessions, which are not in need of currency and are unfamiliar with theaters and gymnasiums. A city without temples and gods, where they don't resort to prayers, oaths, prophecies, or sacrifices for acquiring goods or averting evils—no one has ever been a spectator in such a city, nor will there ever be." (Gnomikologikon- Anthology of Sayings - Library of the Greeks, Vol. 2, published by the Hellenic Publishing Organization, Athens 1972, p. 31).

20.Pythagoras of Samos (580-490 BCE)

He was an important Greek philosopher, mathematician,

geometer, music theorist, and the founder of the Pythagorean School. He is the preeminent founder of Greek mathematics and created a comprehensive system for the science of celestial bodies, supported by all relevant numerical and geometric proofs. He died in Metapontum in Italian Lucania at a ripe old age around 500-490 BCE. Pythagoras' interest in musical harmony led to the attribution of the "Harmony of the Spheres" theory to him. Various geometric discoveries have also been credited to Pythagoras, with his most famous being the Pythagorean Theorem. Finally, he was the first to use the word 'cosmos'.

A «Ἐλεύθερον ἀδύνατον εἶναι τὸν πάθεσι δουλεύοντα καὶ ὑπὸ παθῶν κρατούμενον» (Γνωμικά).

"The one enslaved by passions is impossible to be free and is dominated by those very passions." (Gnomic).

† «Τὰ πάθη ὑποδουλώνουν τὸν ἄνθρωπον» (Ἅγιος Νικόδημος ο Ἁγιορείτης, πηγή: Περιοδικό Πεμπτουσία 18.10.19).

"The passions enslave humanity." (St. Nicodemus the Hagiorite, source: "Pemptousia", October 18, 2019).

A «Μηδένα γὰρ εἶναι σοφὸν ἢ Θεόν» (Διογ. Λαέρτ., Βίοι Φιλοσ. Α12).

"For no one is wise except God alone." (Diogenes Laertius, Lives of the Eminent Philosophers, A12).

† «Μόνῳ σοφῷ Θεῷ (Παύλου, Α΄ Τιμ. α΄,17).

"To the King of the ages, immortal, invisible, the only God, be honor and glory forever and ever. Amen." (1 Timothy 1:17).

† «Ἐν ᾧ (τῷ Θεῷ δηλαδή) πάντες οἱ θησαυροὶ τῆς σοφίας καὶ τῆς γνώσεως ἀπόκρυφοι» (Κολοσσαεῖς β´,3).

"In whom are hidden all the treasures of wisdom and knowledge" (Colossians 2:3).

† «Ὦ βάθος πλούτου καὶ σοφίας καὶ γνώσεως Θεοῦ!» (Ρωμ. ια´, 33).

"Oh, the depth of the riches and wisdom and knowledge of God!" (Romans 11:33).

† «...ἡ πολυποίκιλος σοφία τοῦ Θεοῦ» (Εφεσ. γ´ 10).

"...so that through the church the manifold wisdom of God" (Ephesians 3:10).

† «Ὡς ἐμεγαλύνθη τὰ ἔργα σου Κύριε, πάντα ἐν σοφίᾳ ἐποίησας» (Ψαλμ. ργ´ 24).

"O Lord, how manifold are your works! In wisdom have you made them all;" (Psalm 104:24).

Α «Ῥώμην μεγίστην καὶ πλοῦτον τὴν ἐγκράτειαν κτῆσαι» (Στοβαίου Ανθολόγιον).

"Attain great strength and wealth through self-control." (Florilegium of Stobaeus).

† «Καὶ τὰ μὲν ἀγαθὰ ποὺ προέρχονται ἀπὸ τὴ νηστεία εἶναι τόσα πολλά· ὁ δὲ κορεσμὸς εἶναι ἡ ἀρχὴ τῶν πτώσεων» (Μ. Βασιλείου, Λόγος Α´ για τη νηστεία).

"From fasting come so many good things, but fullness is the beginning of insolence." (St. Basil the Great, 1st Discourse on

Fasting).

† «Οὐ τὸ ἀπέχεσθαι μόνον βρωμάτων ἀληθὴς νηστεία, ἀλλὰ τῶν κακῶν ἀποχή» (αγίου Ιωάννη Χρυσοστόμου).
"The true fasting is not only abstaining from food but also refraining from evil deeds." (St. John Chrysostom).

A «Δικαιοσύνην ἀσκεῖν ἔργῳ τε λόγῳ τε» (Χρυσά Έπη).
"Practice justice in word and deed."(The Golden Verses).

† «Δικαιοσύνην μάθετε οἱ ἐνοικοῦντες ἐπὶ τῆς γῆς» (Από την Ακολουθίαν του Νυμφίου, βλ. Ησ. 26:9.)
"For when your judgments are in the earth, the inhabitants of the world learn righteousness." (Isaiah 26:9).

† «Μακάριοι οἱ πεινῶντες καὶ διψῶντες τὴν δικαιοσύνην ὅτι αὐτοὶ χορτασθήσονται» (Μακαρισμοί, Ματθ. ε',6).
"Blessed are those who hunger and thirst for righteousness, for they shall be satisfied." (Matthew 5:6)

A «Βέλτιστοι γιγνόμεθα πρὸς τοὺς θεοὺς βαδίζοντες» (Γνωμικά).
"We become better by walking in step with the gods." (Gnomic).

† «Ὁ κατοικῶν ἐν βοηθείᾳ τοῦ Ὑψίστου, ἐν σκέπῃ τοῦ Θεοῦ τοῦ οὐρανοῦ αὐλισθήσεται» (Ψαλμός 90).
"He who dwells in the shelter of the Most High will rest in the shadow of the Almighty." (Psalm 91).

A «Σιτία, ποτά, ύπνος, αφροδίσια, πάντα μέτρια». (Χρυσά έπη στίχοι 32-34).

"Food, drinks, sleep, and sexual pleasures, all in moderation." (Golden epics verse 32-34).

† «Έλαμψε της εγκρατείας η ευπρέπεια, των δαιμόνων την αχλύν φυγαδεύουσα, επεδήμησε της νηστείας η σεμνότης, των ψυχικών παθών την ιατρείαν φέρουσα» (Από την υμνολογία του Τριωδίου, της εβδομάδος της Τυρινής).

"The grace of self-control has shone forth, the modesty that banishes the darkness of demons has appeared, the solemnity of fasting has arrived, bringing the cure for the passions of the soul." (Hymnography of the Triodion, from the Week of Tyrophagus).

21.Simonides of Keos (556-468 BCE)

Simonides was an ancient lyric poet and writer of epigrams. He was born in Kea, where he studied poetry and music and composed paeans to Apollo. He traveled to various parts of the Greek world and became associated with the powerful figures of his time, gaining significant economic benefits. He moved to Athens and later to Thessaly. After the Battle of Marathon, he returned to Athens and then went to Sicily, where he died in Acragas or Syracuse in 468 or 469 BCE. He is a distinct example of an intellectual and sensitive poet. With his dithyrambs, which are not preserved, he achieved forty-five victories. His poems are characterized by his rational talent and deep emotion.

A «Πάμπαν δ' ἄμωμος οὔ τις οὐδ' ἀκήριος» (Στοβαίου Ανθολόγιον).

"Absolutely, no one is blameless or without flaw" (Florilegium of Stobaeus).

† «Ὁ ἀναμάρτητος πρῶτος τὸν λίθον βαλέτω» (Ἰω. 8, 7)

"Let him who is without sin among you be the first to throw a stone at her." (John 8:7).

† «Ἐὰν εἴπωμεν ὅτι ἁμαρτίαν οὐκ ἔχομεν ἑαυτοὺς πλανῶμεν. Καὶ ἡ ἀλήθεια οὐκ ἐστιν ἐν ἡμῖν» (Α΄ Ἰω. 1,8).

"If we say we have no sin, we deceive ourselves, and the truth is not in us." (1 John 1:8).

† «Οὐδεὶς γὰρ ἀναμάρτητος εἰ μὴ Σὺ ὁ δυνάμενος καὶ τοῖς μεταστᾶσι δοῦναι τὴν ἀνάπαυσιν» (Κοντάκιον τῶν Κεκοιμημένων).

"For no one is sinless except You, *Who* have power to grant rest to those who have fallen asleep" (Kontakion of the Dormition*)*.

22. Socrates (469-399 BCE)

Philosopher, one of the most significant figures in Greek and global culture. He devoted his entire life to philosophy, teaching not in any formal school but engaging in discussions throughout Athens with people from all walks of life. His main focus was on ethical, religious, social, and political issues. At the age of seventeen, he encountered the philosopher Archelaus, who instilled in him a passion for philosophy. Many, especially young people, observed his philosophical inquiries as he discussed social, political, ethical, and religious matters. Around him, a circle formed, not constituting a school because Socrates did not teach systematically and, unlike the sophists, did not accept payment from his students. In 399 BCE, charges were brought against him, accusing him of impiety toward the gods and corrupting the youth, leading to his condemnation to death. Despite having the opportunity to escape, he chose to obey the laws and drank the poisonous hemlock. Socrates left no writings; what we know about him comes from the works of Xenophon, Plato, and Aristotle.

A «Οὐ τοίνυν μόνον ἤρκεσε τῷ θεῷ τοῦ σώματος ἐπιμεληθῆναι, ἀλλ' ὅπερ μέγιστόν ἐστι καὶ τὴν ψυχὴν κρατίστην τῷ ἀνθρώπῳ ἐνεφύσησε» (Ξενοφῶντος Απομνημονεύματα Α, 4.13).

"Nor was the deity content to care for man's body. What is of yet higher moment, he has implanted in him the noblest type of soul." (Xenophon, Memorabilia of Socrates, 1.4.13).

† « Ἔπλασεν ὁ Θεὸς τὸν ἄνθρωπον, χοῦν ἀπὸ τῆς γῆς, καὶ ἐνεφύσησεν εἰς τὸ πρόσωπον αὐτοῦ πνοὴν ζωῆς, καὶ ἐγένετο ὁ ἄνθρωπος εἰς ψυχὴν ζῶσαν» (Γέν. 2,7).

"Then the LORD God formed the man of dust from the ground and breathed into his nostrils the breath of life, and the man became a living creature." (Genesis 2:7).

† «...γῆθεν μου τὸ σῶμα διέπλασας, δέδωκας δὲ μοι ψυχήν» (Νεκρώσιμον).

"You molded my body from the earth, and you gave me a soul." (Funeral service).

A «Τὸ θεῖον ὅτι τοσοῦτον καὶ τοιοῦτον ἐστί, ὥσθ' ἅμα πάντα ὁρᾶν, καὶ πάντα ἀκούειν καὶ πανταχοῦ παρεῖναι καὶ ἅμα πάντων ἐπιμελεῖσθαι» (Ξενοφῶντος Απομνημονεύματα Α 4, 18 –πηγή: Μπαρακλῆς Χ., σελ.181).

"Such is the greatness and such the nature of the deity that he sees all things and hears all things alike, and is present in all places and heedful of all things." (Xenophon, Memorabilia of Socrates, 1.4.18).

† «ποῦ πορευθῶ ἀπὸ τοῦ πνεύματός σου καὶ ἀπὸ τοῦ προσώπου σου ποῦ φύγω;....» (Ψαλμ. 139:7).

"Where shall I go from your spirit? Or where shall I flee from your presence?" (Psalm 139:7).

23. Solon of Athens (630-560 BCE)

Solon was a great Athenian legislator, philosopher, poet, and one of the Seven Sages of Ancient Greece. He belonged to a wealthy and aristocratic family. Engaging in trade and extensive travels, he acquired not only wealth but also knowledge and wisdom. He studied foreign cultures, laws, as well as their political and economic life, gaining the trust of the public initially as a poet. As a result of the long and violent uprising of the citizens against the nobility, Solon was appointed by the mutual consent of the conflicting parties as the ruler in 594/3 BCE through an exceptional procedure to legislate. For this mission, he was equipped with unlimited powers. The measures he took were bold and strict. As part of the "Seisachtheia"[9] (= shaking off the

---

[9] Etymology of the word:

1. Seisa-: This comes from the Greek verb "seio" (σείω), which means

burdens), he abolished existing debts of private individuals to other private individuals and to the state. He also emancipated Athenians who had become slaves due to debts and abolished lending with the personal freedom of the borrower as collateral. Moreover, he is considered the father of Civil Law.

Α «Τὸ θεῖον καὶ οἱ νόμοι, εὖ μὲν ἀγόντων, εἰσὶν ὠφέλιμοι, κακῶς δὲ ἀγόντων οὐδὲν ὠφελοῦσιν» (Διογ. Λαέρτιος, Βίοι Φιλοσόφων 1.65).

"Divine things and laws, when rightly pursued, are beneficial; but when wrongly pursued, they are of no benefit." (Diogenes Laërtius, Lives of the Eminent Philosophers, 1.65).

† «Πείθεσθε τοῖς ἡγουμένοις ὑμῶν καὶ ὑπείκετε» (Ἑβρ.ιγ′17).

"Obey your leaders and submit to them" (Hebrews 13:17).

Α «Πολλοὶ γὰρ πλουτοῦσι κακοί, ἀγαθοὶ δὲ πένονται, ἀλλ' ἡμεῖς οὐ διαμειψόμεθα τῆς ἀρετῆς τὸν πλοῦτον» (Πλουτάρχου Σόλων 3,3, Ἐλεγεῖαι Θεόγνιδος 315-317).

"Many bad men, for sure, are rich, and many good men poor; yet will we not change our virtue for these men's wealth" (Solon by Plutarch 3.3, The Elegies of Theognis, 315-317).

"to shake" or "to toss." In the context of Seisachtheia, it implies the shaking off or relieving of burdens.

2. -achtheia: This is related to the noun "achthos" (ἄχθος), which means "burden" or "load." The suffix "-theia" indicates a process or action, so "-achtheia" suggests the action of removing burdens.

† «Ἀμὴν λέγω ὑμῖν ὅτι πλούσιος δυσκόλως εἰσελεύσεται εἰς τὴν Βασιλείαν τῶν Οὐρανῶν» (Ματθ. 19, 23).

"Truly, I say to you, only with difficulty will a rich person enter the kingdom of heaven." (Matthew 19:23).

Α «Μὴ ψεύδου, ἀλλ᾿ ἀλήθευε» (Στοβαίου Ανθολόγιον).

"Do not lie, but speak the truth." (Florilegium of Stobaeus).

† «Οὐ ψευδομαρτυρήσεις κατὰ τοῦ πλησίον σου μαρτυρίαν ψευδῆ» (9η εντολή).

"You must not testify falsely against your neighbor." (9th Commandment).

Α «Χρῶ τοῖς Θεοῖς» (Στοβαίου Ανθολόγιον).

"Commune with the gods" (Florilegium of Stobaeus).

† «Πᾶσαν τὴν ζωὴν ἡμῶν Χριστῷ τῷ Θεῷ παραθώμεθα» (Λειτουργικόν).

"Let us commend ourselves and one another, and our whole life to Christ our God." (Liturgy).

Α «Θεοὺς τίμα, γονέας αἰδοῦ» (Γνωμικολογικόν).

"Honor the gods, respect your parents." (Gnomikologikon – Anthology of Sayings).

† «Ἐγώ εἰμι Κύριος ὁ Θεός σου. Οὐκ ἔσονταί σοι Θεοὶ ἕτεροι πλὴν ἐμοῦ» (1η εντολή).

"I am the LORD your God. You shall have no other gods before Me." (1ˢᵗ Commandment).

✝ «Τίμα τὸν πατέρα σου καὶ τὴν μητέρα σου, ἵνα εὖ σοι γένηται καὶ ἵνα μακροχρόνιος ἔσῃ ἐπὶ τῆς γῆς τῆς ἀγαθῆς, ἧς Κύριος ὁ Θεός σου δίδωσί σοι» (5η εντολή).

"Honor your father and your mother, as the LORD your God commanded you, that your days may be long, and that it may go well with you in the land that the LORD your God is giving you." (5ᵗʰ Commandment).

24. Sophocles (496-406 BCE)

He was an ancient Greek tragic poet, the second among the three greatest tragedians of the 5th century BCE. Born in Colonus to a wealthy family, he received a comprehensive education. From childhood, he excelled in the competitions of Music and Gymnastics. He learned the art of tragedy from Aeschylus. He triumphed over his teacher in his debut as a dramatic poet in the 468 BCE competition. He took an interest in political affairs and was honored by the Athenians. In fact, following the presentation of "Antigone," they elected him as a general in the war against the Samians (441-439 BCE). He received other distinctions, including a priesthood. He composed one hundred twenty-three dramas, elegies, and paeans and he surpassed Aeschylus and Euripides in victories at dramatic competitions. Only seven of his tragedies have survived.

Α «Ἄνθρωπός ἐστι πνεῦμα καὶ σκιὰ μόνον» (Στοβαίου Ανθολόγιον, από το έργο Αίας Λοκρός).

"A human being is only a breath and a shadow."
(Florilegium of Stobaeus, from Ajax the Locrian).

† « Ἄνθρωπος ματαιότητι ὁμοιώθη, αἱ ἡμέραι αὐτοῦ ὡσεὶ σκιὰ παράγουσι» (Ψαλμ. 143,4).
"Man is like a breath; his days are like a passing shadow" (Psalm 144:4).

† «Ὡς ἄνθος μαραίνεται καὶ ὡς ὄναρ παρέρχεται καὶ διαλύεται πᾶς ἄνθρωπος» (Νεκρώσιμον).
"As a flower withers, as a dream passes, so every human dissolves" (Funeral service).

Α «Οὗτοι συνέχθειν ἀλλὰ συμφιλεῖν ἔφυν» (Ἀντιγόνη, στίχ. 523, Γνωμικά).
"I was born, not to hate, but to love." (Antigone, 523).

† «Ταῦτα ἐντέλλομαι ὑμῖν ἵνα ἀγαπᾶτε ἀλλήλους» (Ἰωάν. ιε΄, 17).
"These things I command you, so that you will love one another." (John 15:17).

25. Thales of Miletus (625-546 BCE)

Thales, one of the Seven Sages of ancient Greece, is primarily considered by Aristotle and other ancient philosophers as the first Greek philosopher chronologically. He discovered solstices, the phases of the Moon, as well as electricity and magnetism, deriving from the attractive properties of the mineral magnet and amber. Thales is also known for successfully predicting the solar eclipse of 585 BCE. He attempted to comprehend the world through the lens of science and explain natural phenomena without relying on references to mythology, as was common until his time. Thales believed that the world is full of gods[10] and that the soul is something movable[11]. Essentially, this represents an archaic expression of the theory of hylozoism, asserting that the world is alive and ensouled, substantiated by its inherent motion.

A «Τί τὸ θεῖον; Τὸ μήτε ἀρχὴν μήτε τέλος ἔχον» (Στοβαίου Ανθολόγιον).

"What is divine? That which has neither beginning nor end." (Florilegium of Stobaeus).

† «Ὁ Θεὸς ὁ ἄναρχος καὶ ἀτελεύτητος, ὁ πάσης κτίσεως πρεσβύτατος ὑπάρχων» *(Από τη χειροτονία πρεσβυτέρου)*.

"God, the beginningless and endless, being the eldest of all creation" (From the ordination of a presbyter).

A «Κάλλιστον ὁ κόσμος. Ποίημα γὰρ θεοῦ» (Διογ. Λαέρτιος, *Βίοι Φιλοσόφων* Α35, Γνωμικά).

"The world is most beautiful. For it is a work of God." (Diogenes Laërtius, Lives of the Eminent Philosophers, A35, Gnomic).

† «Καὶ εἶδεν ὁ Θεὸς τὰ πάντα, ὅσα ἐποίησε, καὶ ἰδοὺ καλὰ λίαν» *(Γεν.* 1,31).

---

[10] «πάντα πλήρη θεῶν εἶναι»

[11] «κινητικόν τι»

"And God saw everything that he had made, and behold, it was very good" (Genesis 1:31).

Α «Πρεσβύτερον τῶν ὄντων ὁ Θεός, ἀγέννητον γάρ» (Διογ. Λαέρτ., *Βίοι Φιλοσ.* Α35, Γνωμικά).

"The oldest of things is God, for He is unborn." (Diogenes Laërtius, Lives of the Eminent Philosophers, A35, Gnomic).

† «Ὁ Θεὸς εἶναι ἄναρχος καὶ ἀτελεύτητος» (*Ἅγιος Ἰωάννης Δαμασκηνός*).

"God is without beginning and without end." (St. John of Damascus).

26. Xenophanes of Colophon (570-475 BCE)

Xenophanes was a philosopher and poet born in the Anatolian city of Colophon, who lived in various places of the ancient Greek world. The image of Xenophanes that emerges from the remaining fragments presents him as a traveling rhapsode who challenged and criticized the poetic depictions of the gods, introducing a new conception of divine nature. Additionally, he was a thoughtful observer of human nature and an advocate of a specific form of inquiry (Historiae), which was adopted by the Milesian philosophers and scholars of his time. Simultaneously, his work as a rhapsode made him a social advisor to his fellow citizens, urging them to respect divine nature and protect the well-being of their city. He spent time in Catania, Sicily, where he engaged with Homer and Hesiod. There, he wrote his own works and composed poems about the founding of Colophon and Elea. Later writers added that he "buried his sons with his own hands," was sold as a slave, and was freed at an old age. History remembers him for his criticism of anthropomorphic religious representations, his promotion of monotheism through his thinking, and some pioneering ideas in various fields of knowledge.

Α «Ἐκ γαίης γὰρ πάντα καὶ εἰς γῆν πάντα τελευτᾶ» *(Γνωμικά).*

"For all things come from earth, and all things end by becoming earth." (Gnomic).

† «Γῆ εἶ καὶ εἰς γῆν ἀπελεύσει» *(Νεκρώσιμος ακολουθία, βλ. Γεν 3,19).*

"For you are dust, and to dust you shall return" (Genesis 3:19).

Α «Πάντες γαίης τε καὶ ὕδατος ἐκγενόμεθα» *(Γνωμικά).*

"We all come from earth and water." (Gnomic).

† «Ἐμνήσθη ὅτι χοῦς ἐσμέν» *(Ψαλμ. 102, 14).*

"For he knows our frame; he remembers that we are dust." (Psalm 103:14).

† «Γῆθέν μου τὸ σῶμα διέπλασας» *(Νεκρώσιμο).*

"You molded my body from the earth." (Funeral Service).

Α «Εἷς Θεὸς ἔν τε θεοῖσι καὶ ἀνθρώποισι μέγιστος οὔτε δέμας θνητοῖσι ὅμοιος οὐδὲ νόημα». *(Αγίου Νεκταρίου, Ἅπαντα, Η′ σελ. 28)*

"One god greatest among gods and men, not at all like mortals in body or in thought." (St Nektarios, Apanta/Complete Works, vol.

H', p.28).

† «Θεὸν οὐδεὶς ἑώρακε πώποτε» (Ἰω. α',18).
"No one has ever seen God" (John 1:18).

† «Πνεῦμα ὁ Θεὸς καὶ τοὺς προσκυνοῦντας αὐτὸν ἐν πνεύματι καὶ ἀληθείᾳ δεῖ προσκυνεῖν» (Ἰω. δ', 24).
"God is spirit and those who worship Him must worship in spirit and truth (John, 4:24).

27.Xenophon (430-355 BCE)

Xenophon (Erchia, 430 BC - Corinth, 355 BC) was an Athenian historian and Socratic philosopher. The son of Gryllus from the ancient deme of Erchia (modern-day Spata), he belonged socially to the class of horsemen and was politically active as an oligarch and philo-Laconian. After 410 BC, he became acquainted with Socrates and joined his circle of students. Xenophon developed a rich and varied activity. In the field of historiography, with his work "Hellenica," divided into seven books, he continued the work of Thucydides, covering the period from 411 BC to 361 BC. Of more general significance for political philosophy is "Cyropaedia," in 8 books, where, in the spirit of sophistic and Socratic ideology and with the model of the slightly historical and highly fictionalized portrayal of the founder of the Persian Empire, Cyrus the Great, he composes the image of the ideal monarch.

Α «Σὺν θεοῖς οὐδενός ἀπορήσομεν» (Γνωμικά).
"With the gods with us, we will lack nothing." (Gnomic).

† «Πλούσιοι ἐπτώχευσαν καὶ ἐπείνασαν, οἱ δὲ ἐκζητοῦντες τὸν Κύριον οὐκ ἐλαττωθήσονται παντὸς ἀγαθοῦ» (Ψαλμ. 33,11).

"The young lions suffer want and hunger, but those who seek the Lord lack no good thing." (Psalm 34:10).

Α «Τὸ θεῖον (...) πάντα ὁρᾶν καὶ πάντα ἀκούειν καὶ πανταχοῦ παρεῖναι...» (Ξενοφ. Απομνημονεύματα 1.4.18, πηγή: Μπαρακλῆς Χ. Γνωμικά καὶ Παροιμίαι, σελ. 181).

"The divine sees and hears everything at once and is present everywhere." (Xenophon's "Memorabilia" 1.4.18, source: Baraklis, Ch., Proverbs and Sayings, p.181).

† «(Ὁ Θεὸς) πανταχοῦ παρών» (Από την προσευχή «Βασιλεῦ οὐράνιε»).

"God is omnipresent" (From the prayer "O Heavenly King").

BIBLIOGRAPHICAL REFERENCES*

1. Holy Scripture
2. Saint Nektarios (Kefalas), Complete Works, Volume E (Treasury of Sacred and Philosophical Sayings), © 1896.
3. Diogenes Laërtius, Lives of the Eminent Philosophers. Editor: Madelaras V. Cactus publishing, © 1994, ISBN 9789603523062.
4. Baraklis Char., Maxims and Proverbs, Publisher: Estia Bookstore - I.D. Kollarou & Co, © 2008. ISBN 9789600500301.
5. Gerontikon, Patristic Texts, Church Hymnography, etc. (https://glt.goarch.org/).
6. Pausanias, Description of Greece, Phocis, Locrians. Cactus publishing, © 2005.
7. Plevris K. "Οι Έλληνες" Ηλεκτρον publications 2017 p.101.
8. Sarikakis Theod., The Oldest University in the World, from the Scientific Yearbook of the Philosophy School of the National and Kapodistrian University of Athens, Volume LA (1996-1997)

---

* While not all of these books have been translated into English, the titles presented herein are transcribed from the original Greek into English for the benefit of readers interested in conducting further research.

9. Florilegium of Stobaeus, Georgiadis Publishers, ISBN 960-316-260-4

10. Tziropoulou-Efstathiou Anna, Archaeognosia, Issue No. 22/75

11. Tsinikopoulos Dimitris, Ancient Greek Philosophers on God (online source https://tsinikopoulos.org/).

12. Nicodemus the Hagiorite: Synaxarist of the twelve months of the year, Volume A, Domos publications 2005

ONLINE SOURCES

1. www.perseus.tufts.edu
2. Wikisource (wikisource.org)
3. Gnomic (Γνωμικά) at: Gnomikologikon.gr
4. Pemptousia.gr
5. www.evripidis.gr/product/53939/alkidamas-ritorika-anonyma-793-/
6. Πέτρος Ιωαννίδης, Ἐξ Ἱππαρχίας*, Ἱππαρχισμοῦ* ἄρχεσθαι & Ἀν-ιππαρχίας* παύεσθαι, www.ebdomi.com/arthra-apopseis/12665-ex-ipparxias-ipparxismou-arxesthai-kai-an-ipparxias-pavesthai.html
7. el.wikipedia.org/wiki/Ἀρχίλοχος
8. www.gnomikologikon.gr/authquotes.php?auth=5
9. el.wikipedia.org/wiki Χίλων_ο_Λακεδαιμόνιος
10. el.wikipedia.org/wiki/ Κλεόβουλος
11. el.wikipedia.org/wiki/ Δημόκριτος
12. el.wikipedia.org/wiki/Ἐπίκτητος,
13. https://www.kaktos.gr/el/ta-apanta-tou-epiktitou.html?gad_source=1&gclid=CjwKCAjw0YGyBhBy EiwAQmBEWsxvsNS05pWAFJMqSUsYMnQ8ZLpGC7Bq SJO-eKo9d4wb73RrsyN-JhoCBxoQAvD_BwE
14. el.wikipedia.org/wiki/Ευριπίδης
15. www.gnomikologikon.gr/authquotes.php?auth=40
16. el.wikipedia.org/wiki/Ἱπποκράτης
17. el.wikiquote.org/wiki/Ὅμηρος

18. el.wikipedia.org/wiki/Όμηρος
19. el.wikipedia.org/wiki/Ισοκράτης
20. el.wikipedia.org/wiki/Φωκυλίδης
21. el.wikipedia.org/wiki/Πλούταρχος
22. el.wikipedia.org/wiki/Πυθαγόρας
23. el.wikipedia.org/wiki/Πιττακός
24. el.wikipedia.org/wiki/Σιμωνίδης_ο_Κείος
25. www.gnomikologikon.gr/authquotes.php?auth=3
26. el.wikipedia.org/wiki/Σόλων_ο_Αθηναίος
27. el.wikipedia.org/wiki/Ξενοφάνης
28. el.wikipedia.org/wiki/Ξενοφών

ABOUT THE AUTHOR

Vasileios Bellios was born in 1937 in Greece, in the small village of Tzivas in Arcadia. He studied medicine at the University of Vienna in Austria where he also obtained a doctorate. Following the completion of his military service in Greece, he returned to Vienna, and specialized in obstetrics and gynecology.

He eventually returned to Greece where he excelled as a dedicated medical professional, helping women and successfully delivering over 5000 babies. While practicing his profession, he has also been involved in providing lectures on the subject of Greece's demographics, fertility, and human relationships, in several parent associations, and schools throughout Greece. He is married to Anastasia Papandrianou, a teacher of English literature, and has three children, two sons, and a daughter.

Fluent in German but with a profound appreciation and interest in his native language, Greek, Vasileios has studied the ancient Greek Philosophers. He has always been interested and amazed by their profound intellect and finds their teachings more current than ever.